ALCATRAZ

PRISON FOR AMERICA'S MOST WANTED

NONFICTION BY
C. J. HENDERSON

SCHOLASTIC INC.
**New York   Toronto   London   Auckland   Sydney
Mexico City   New Delhi   Hong Kong**

CRIMINALS ON THE COVER

TOP ROW, LEFT TO RIGHT

B. PAUL COY, LOUIS LEPKE BUCHALTER, GEORGE "MACHINE GUN" KELLY
(AP/WIDE WORLD, ARCHIVE PHOTOS, AP/WIDE WORLD)

MIDDLE ROW, LEFT TO RIGHT

JOHN ANGLIN, AL CAPONE, FRANK LEE MORRIS
(ALL PHOTOS ARE AP/WIDE WORLD)

BOTTOM ROW, LEFT TO RIGHT

DUTCH SCHULTZ, FRED BARKER, CLARENCE ANGLIN
(ARCHIVE PHOTOS, AP/WIDE WORLD, ARCHIVE PHOTOS)

Copyright © 1999 by Scholastic Inc.
All rights reserved. Published by Scholastic Inc.
Printed in the U.S.A.

ISBN 0-439-05673-X

SCHOLASTIC, READ 180, and associated logos and designs are trademarks and/or registered trademarks of Scholastic Inc.
LEXILE is a trademark of MetaMetrics, Inc.

6   7   8   9   10   23   06   05

TABLE OF CONTENTS

It was the 1920s in America. Police were fighting crime everywhere. Gangsters were shooting it out on the streets. Robbers were stealing from each other. Many ordinary Americans were breaking the law every day.

Much of this crime began when a new law was passed. This law made it illegal to make, sell, or drink alcohol. It was called the National Prohibition Act.

How did this law lead to a crime wave?

Even though it was against the law, many people still wanted to buy alcohol.

So criminals took over. They saw a new way to make money—lots of it. Some started sneaking alcohol in from other countries. Others made their own.

Illegal bars opened. You could find them everywhere. Before Prohibition, New York City had 15,000 bars. After the new law, 32,000 illegal ones took their place.

The criminals made huge profits. Some of them lived like kings. They paid local police and politicians to leave them alone. They murdered the ones they could not bribe.

Even when these men were caught, nothing changed. They ruled from jail. They paid guards to pass messages for them. If the guards said no, the gangsters threatened to hurt their families.

The gangsters laughed at justice. Even in jail they couldn't be stopped. Alcohol was on every corner. Crime was wild in the streets.

Then a man named Homer C. Cummings came up with an idea.

His idea involved an island.

The island's name was Alcatraz.

The super-prison would keep the toughest prisoners locked up for good.

THE SUPER-PRISON 1

Homer C. Cummings had a tough job. He had to stop the gangsters. He had to get them into jail. But that was only the first step. He also had to cut them off from the outside world.

Cummings decided he needed a "super-prison for super-prisoners." Once inside, the gangsters wouldn't be able to talk to their men on the outside. They wouldn't be able to threaten guards' families. They would be put away once and for all.

Cummings decided Alcatraz was the place. It was a big, rocky island. It sat far out in California's San Francisco Bay. The nearest land was over a mile away. The water around it was cold all year. The currents were too powerful for swimmers. And there was an old prison on the island already.

Cummings was given five years to make his idea work. He hired a man named James Johnston as the first warden. Johnston started work right away.

First, he made the old buildings stronger. He replaced old iron bars with steel ones.

Then he added new buildings.

Telephones and radios came next. That way the guards could talk to each other from any point on the island.

Tall guard towers were built around the prison. Each had huge searchlights.

Tear gas came next. If prisoners rioted, the guards could drop gas from slots in the ceiling.

Then the gun boxes were built. They were steel boxes set high on the walls. Guards would sit inside. They pointed machine guns through small holes. And they kept watch 24 hours a day.

Next, electric gates and doors were added. Guards could lock any part of the jail just by pushing a button.

Metal detectors were placed everywhere. Prisoners would pass through them at least eight times a day.

Barbed wire went on all the fences.

Johnston then built one main control center. It was open only to the outside. All the weapons were kept there.

A single man stayed in the control center. Dozens of microphones were placed around the prison. This man could hear every sound in Alcatraz. He also knew if any phone was off the hook for 15 seconds. He could send a guard to find out if anything was wrong.

Guards counted the prisoners 12 times a day and reported to the man in the control center. If anyone was missing, he called for help.

Finally, guards were hired. Johnston picked them carefully from other prisons.

They were expert shots. They knew judo and other forms of self-defense. They were tough.

There were a lot of them, too. There was one guard for every three prisoners. Most prisons had just one for every ten prisoners.

Guards stood in the towers and at every door. They watched the roads and the stairs.

The guards and their families had to live on the island. Their kids even went to school there. There was no way any gangster could threaten a guard's family.

By August 18, 1934, "The Rock" was open for business.

It was time for the prisoners.

Why was it so important to build a strong prison? What made this prison so tough?

Prisoners arrived at Alcatraz. And they found out that it was the toughest prison ever.

PRISON LIFE 2

Reporters were full of questions about the first prisoners. But no one was talking. The operation was top-secret.

Where were the prisoners coming from? No answer.

When would they arrive? No answer.

Was Al Capone, the most famous gangster of all, coming to Alcatraz? Johnston said he was not. (He was.)

Johnston had one big fear. The prisoners would arrive by train from all around the country. Each train would be packed with the most terrible criminals alive. Gangsters might attack the trains. The gang leaders could be set free . . . if their friends knew where they were.

At midnight on August 18, the prison in Atlanta, Georgia, was quiet. A special train moved through the darkness into the yard.

Guards made 53 prisoners leave the jail. Each had his legs and wrists chained. They moved into the train. When they were chained to their seats, the train pulled off.

The train reached San Francisco several days later. Even then, the prisoners did not get off. A special boat had been built. The train was driven right onto the boat. Then the train was taken to the island. Warden Johnston was taking no chances.

More trains soon arrived. The prisoners quickly learned about Alcatraz.

For the first few years, prisoners couldn't even speak to each other. They could ask for salt at a meal. They could ask for a tool at work. But that was it. Sometimes guards caught prisoners talking. Those prisoners ended up in the cellar.

Prisoners called the cellar the "Hole." It was a group of small cells under the prison. Prisoners were chained to a brick wall. They stayed there 24 hours a day in the dark.

There was no one else in sight. They were fed bread and water. Every 19 days they could have a shower. They could be in the Hole for ten days, a month, or even a year.

Every day on the Rock was the same. Prisoners got up at 6 A.M. They washed with cold water. They put on gray shirts and pants.

They marched to breakfast. There was plenty of food, and it was good. But prisoners who left food on their plates had to skip the next meal. The next time it happened they were sent to the Hole for 10 days.

The rest of the day was spent working and eating. On Sunday, prisoners got a two-hour break in the yard. They could go to church in the morning. But if they did, they got less time in the yard.

Day after day passed. Each one was the same. No one spoke. No radios played. Visitors were allowed only once a month. And a guard was always there, listening.

This life drove some prisoners crazy. A prisoner named Al Loomis spent 16 months on Alcatraz. "It's driving the men nuts," Loomis said. "The walls were the barest things I ever saw. If a man tried to put up a photo of his mother he was headed for the Hole. They never give a guy a break."

Warden Johnston thought his rules were working. "We have some tough customers," he said. "But we have torn them down to size. We have [made them realize] that they are not as big as they thought they were."

What were Johnston's goals? Do you think he met these goals?

Alvin Karpis was Public Enemy #1. Could Alcatraz keep him behind bars?

OLD CREEPY 3

Who were the criminals inside Alcatraz?

One of the Rock's biggest catches was Alvin "Old Creepy" Karpis.

Alvin started his life of crime by breaking into stores at night. He was ten years old.

As a teenager, he helped other criminals sell the things they stole.

Then he met Freddie Barker.

Freddie took Karpis home to meet his mother. She was known as Ma Barker. She liked the sour, creepy-looking boy. So she gave him his nickname.

Karpis spent many years robbing and killing and kidnapping with the Barkers. Then he started robbing banks on his own.

He also thought of a new crime. He'd rob

trains. No one had robbed a train in America in years. The Federal Bureau of Investigation (FBI) was proud of that, too. Karpis looked forward to making them mad.

And he did. J. Edgar Hoover, the head of the FBI, was furious. He swore he'd capture Karpis. Old Creepy just laughed.

It seemed like Karpis would never be caught. He shot his way out of more than one police trap. He was Public Enemy #1.

Finally, the FBI found Karpis in New Orleans. Hoover flew there to arrest him. Many agents surrounded Karpis's house. When he came out to his car, they jumped him.

Hoover ordered his men to handcuff Karpis. But none of the agents had remembered their handcuffs. They used a necktie to tie him up. Old Creepy just laughed.

Karpis was put in jail for life. He said that he could escape from any prison. But in 1937, he entered Alcatraz. In 1962, he was still there. The Rock had beaten him.

Robert Stroud was sent to prison for life. And there he learned all he could about birds.

THE BIRDMAN 4

Robert Stroud killed a man when he was 19. He was sent to prison for 12 years.

Just before Stroud's sentence was over, he stabbed a guard. No one knows why. He was sent to a prison in Kansas for life.

One day Stroud found a nest of sparrows in the exercise yard. He took the baby birds to his cell. He gave them bits of bread. And he nursed them back to health.

Stroud became very interested in birds. He read all the books on birds in the prison library.

He brought more birds into his cell. He fed them flies and bits of his own meals. He built cages for his birds from a box. He used a

ALCATRAZ

AP/WIDE WORLD

Here's one of the eight gun towers at Alcatraz. Guards kept watch 24 hours a day. They were in constant contact with the main control center of the prison.

An Alcatraz guard operates a metal detector in 1956. Every visitor had to pass through it.

This guard is working in the control center of the prison. He guarded all the guns, tear gas, and bullets. The control center was lined with thick, bullet-proof glass. The guard had the only key to the room.

Inside Alcatraz: prisoners' cells are on the left. There were guards with guns behind the screens on the right.

Here's where prisoners ate. The food was good. But if prisoners did not finish a meal, they had to skip the next one.

The prison hospital: see the bars on the windows? Even the sick weren't trusted!

This is a prisoner's cell. Prisoners spent most of their time here. They were rarely allowed to talk. They couldn't listen to music. They could have visitors only once a month. They could leave their cells to eat and take showers. On Sundays, they got a break in the yard. Or they could go to church.

ESCAPE FROM ALCATRAZ

Frank Morris, John and Clarence Anglin *(left to right)*.

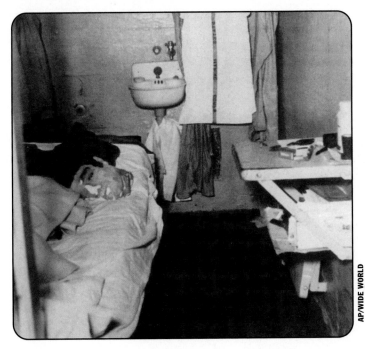

The three men above escaped in 1962. To fool the guards, they left fake heads in their beds.

THE PRISONERS

Here's Karpis after more than 30 years at Alcatraz.

One of Alcatraz's "super-prisoners" was "Old Creepy" Karpis. He was arrested for kidnapping in 1933.

Capone, after 5 years in Alcatraz.

Al Capone was one of the most powerful criminals in America. He was responsible for more than 1,000 murders. Here he is in 1936, before prison.

Robert Stroud became an expert on birds *before* he came to Alcatraz.

A shot from the movie, *Birdman of Alcatraz*. Stroud was actually not allowed to have birds there.

This photo of Alcatraz was taken from a plane. The island is surrounded by San Francisco Bay. The nearest land is a mile away.

The prison opened in 1934. It closed in 1963. Only a few people ever escaped from "The Rock." But no one knows if they lived to tell about it.

broken razor blade and an old nail for tools.

Stroud studied birds for years. He even wrote two books on bird illnesses. Few people in the world knew more about the diseases of birds.

Stroud was moved to Alcatraz a few years after it opened. He wasn't allowed to have birds there. He became known as the "Birdman of Alcatraz" anyway.

Many people tried to get Stroud released because of his work with birds. They wrote letters. They formed protests. No one listened. Once Alcatraz got its hold on a prisoner, it never let go.

Robert Stroud died while still in prison. He was 76 years old. He spent 56 of those years behind bars.

More than 40 of them were on the Rock.

Capone was the most powerful gangster in the world. Could he be stopped?

AL CAPONE 5

The Rock's most famous prisoner was Al Capone. By the age of 26, Capone was the king of Chicago's gang world. In fact, he was the most powerful criminal in the world.

Capone sold alcohol to millions of drinkers. And his business made him very rich. He was making about $5 million a year.

Capone was a very violent man. He was responsible for more than 1,000 murders. Capone ordered the deaths of policemen, politicians, and gangsters. He killed anyone who got in his way. He murdered many of them himself. He would kill his own men if they didn't obey him.

Capone ran Chicago. He paid the police

and politicians to do what he said. Most of them obeyed him without questions.

One time the mayor of Cicero, Illinois, did not obey Capone. Capone found the mayor on the steps of City Hall. He beat him up in broad daylight. Policemen just stood around. They turned their backs. They pretended they didn't see a thing.

Finally, the U.S. government came after Capone. They could not prove that he had murdered anyone. There was no one brave enough to tell on Capone.

So the government brought Capone to trial for not paying his taxes. He was sentenced to 10 years in prison.

Capone started his term in a prison in Georgia. There, he bribed guards. They did him special favors. They brought him good meals and fine cigars. He spent his days eating, smoking, relaxing, and listening to the radio.

Then one night he was ordered out of his cell. Guards searched him. They chained him and pushed him onto a train. Several days later, Capone had a new home: Alcatraz.

Life was never the same for Capone. The silence drove him crazy. His first week there he tried to talk during a meal. He got 10 days in the Hole.

When he got out of the Hole, he wanted to talk about it. He got another 10 days.

A week after that, he tried to bribe a guard for news. That got him 19 days.

Capone had no power in Alcatraz. He couldn't get special favors. He ate prison food. He had no cigars. There was no radio. He had to clean toilets.

In the end, Capone became insane. He would not come out of his cell. He spent hours making and remaking his bed.

In 1940, Capone was freed. He died a few years later. He was powerless and forgotten.

Alcatraz had destroyed him.

Many people tried to escape from Alcatraz. But did anyone ever make it?

ESCAPE! 6

Warden Johnston wanted to make it impossible to escape from Alcatraz. And he may have succeeded. Most people think that no one ever escaped the Rock.

Not alive anyway.

Teddy Cole was a murderer and a kidnapper. He was sent to Alcatraz for 50 years. When he arrived, he said, "I don't think I'll like it here. I doubt I'll stay long."

He didn't. In December 1937, he teamed up with a bank robber named Ralph Roe.

They sawed the bars off a window. They kicked out two panes of glass. They dropped to the ground in a heavy fog. Then they smashed a lock on the fence gate. They jumped 20 feet off a cliff. Then they jumped another 30 feet into San Francisco Bay.

They were never seen again. But this did not mean they escaped. The water was freezing that day. And the current was running fast. Most people assume the two men were washed out to sea.

John and Clarence Anglin were brothers. They were both sent to Alcatraz. In 1962, John, Clarence, and their friend Frank Morris decided to escape.

They spent months digging holes through the back walls of their cells. When the prison first opened, its walls were in perfect condition. But after 25 years, the salt air had worn them down. Now they could be chipped away with a spoon!

The three men had planned their escape perfectly. They worked at night. They were very careful.

Guards counted the prisoners' heads

during the night. So the prisoners saved newspaper, wire, paint, and their own hair. They made models of their own heads. Then they put the fake heads in their beds at night to fool the guards.

Next, they replaced the metal air grates in their cells with fake grates. They made these out of cardboard. They hid their tools in a empty hall behind the walls. They hid their escape equipment there as well.

By the summer, they had dug their way through the walls. Then they made their move. On the night of June 11, 1962, the three climbed into the hidden hallway. They climbed from floor to floor behind the cells.

They made their way to the roof. On the roof, they headed to the north of the island. Then they slipped into the water. They paddled away on a raft made out of raincoats. And like Ralph Roe and Teddy Cole, they disappeared.

Did they make it? No one knows. No bodies were ever found. The current was slow that day. But the water was cold. And land was a mile and a half away.

Besides, these men had never been able to stay out of trouble. They were never arrested again. So it seems unlikely that they made it.

But no one will ever know for sure.

Do you think that John, Clarence, and Frank made it to San Francisco? Why or why not?

For two terrifying days, the criminals took over.
And the guards became prisoners.

RIOT!

Most of the escape attempts at Alcatraz were very quiet. They ended without much violence. Then Bernie Coy tried to escape.

Coy was a bank robber from Kentucky. The guards didn't think he was dangerous. So they made him a janitor. He was allowed to go where other prisoners couldn't go.

It was Thursday, May 2, 1946. Coy was pushing a broom quietly around a cell block. A cell block is a group of cells. Coy's partner was also cleaning nearby.

Bert Burch, a guard, sat in the gun box above. Officer W.H. Miller was on duty in the cell block.

At exactly 1:40 P.M., Burch walked into a

walled-off section of the gun box. Coy had a plan. At the right moment, he knocked on the cell-block door. Miller came to the door. Coy hit him from behind. The partner knocked him out. They locked him in a cell and took his keys.

A couple of prisoners lifted Coy to the gun gallery. He climbed to its roof and worked his way in. When Burch came back, Coy hit him with a club. Coy took a pistol and a rifle. Then he released the rest of the prisoners.

Coy and several others headed for the door to the prison yard. Coy planned to break into the yard. Then he and his friends would go to the prison boat. They would disappear into San Francisco.

But there was one problem. The key to the door of the yard was gone. Miller had taken it off his key ring. Coy and his friends could not get outside. They could not get to the boat.

Coy returned to the cell block. A riot began.

For 48 hours, the prisoners ruled The Rock. They terrified the guards they had captured.

Finally, U.S. Marines were sent in. They stormed the island and took control of the prison.

Many prisoners died in the riot. Coy and two of his friends died. One of his friends was given 99 more years in prison. The other two were killed in the gas chamber. Two guards died.

It was the only riot in the history of Alcatraz.

Today, people from all over the world come to see Alcatraz.

THE ROCK TODAY

Alcatraz was the most successful prison ever built in America. The Rock held the most dangerous prisoners alive. And it kept them safely locked away.

But in 1963, the Rock opened its doors. The prisoners were shipped to jails around the country. The problem: Alcatraz was too expensive to run. It cost twice as much as any other federal prison.

Since Alcatraz was an island, supplies had to be brought over on boats. Even fresh drinking water arrived by boat.

Frank Morris and the Anglin brothers had something to do with the closing, too. Their escape shook prison officials and the public. They had dug through the walls with a spoon.

The Rock was falling apart. And it was too expensive to fix.

Many people also felt that there was no need for a super-prison. Prohibition had ended in 1933. The gangsters seemed under control.

On March 21, 1963, the government shut down the Rock. Nine years later, Alcatraz became a park. Today, visitors from all over the world come to see it.

You can walk in and hear the doors close behind you.

Then, when you get tired of the Rock, you can make your escape.

Why do you think people like to visit Alcatraz?

DID YOU LIKE THIS BOOK?

Here are two other READ 180 Paperbacks that you might like to read.

20,000 LEAGUES UNDER THE SEA
Three men are trapped in a submarine with a madman. Will they ever escape? Or will they spend the rest of their lives in this underwater prison?
BY ADAM GRANT AND TERRY M. WEST
BASED ON THE NOVEL BY JULES VERNE

FINDING THE *TITANIC*
On April 10, 1912, the *Titanic* set sail. On April 15, this great ship sank. Many years later, a scientist discovered the wreck. In this book, he tells the story of the ship and of his discovery.
BY ROBERT BALLARD

GLOSSARY

bribe   to offer someone money to do a special favor for you

cellar   a room below the ground level of a house or building

criminal   someone who commits a crime

current   the movement of water in a river or ocean

detectors   machines used to find something, such as metal or smoke

gangster   a member of a gang of criminals

grates   grids of metal bars that cover something

illegal   against the law

judo   a sport in which two people fight each other, using quick, controlled movements, each trying to throw the other to the ground

politicians   people who run for or hold a government office

Prohibition In this book, it refers to a law passed in 1920 that made it illegal to make, drink, or sell alcoholic drinks in the United States.

sentence punishment given to a person found guilty of a crime

threaten tell someone that harm will be done

violent showing or caused by great physical force or by very strong feeling

warden someone in charge of a prison